COWBOYS

ROUNDUP ON AN AMERICAN RANCH

COWBOYS

ROUNDUP ON AN AMERICAN RANCH

BY JOAN ANDERSON   PHOTOGRAPHS BY GEORGE ANCONA

 SCHOLASTIC INC. · NEW YORK

The seed of this book as well as its creative impulse came from our editor, Tim Peck. We are truly grateful for his energy and guidance.

What a privilege to be taken in by the Larry Eby family of Faywood, New Mexico. Their hospitality, informality, and willingness to show us all sides of ranching were the inspiration for this book. They are truly good neighbors to mankind! Their sons, Leedro and Colter, were patient in answering all our questions and helping us ride horses and survive the days on the range. To be part of such wholesome honesty is rare, and we are deeply grateful.

This book was also made possible because of the introductions made by the Silver City Historical Society, most particularly Robin Jillian. Her contacts and advice were invaluable.

And finally, thanks to all the cowboys: Abe Chacon, Oscar Chacon, Randy Biebelle, his wife Nina and son Brandon, Billy Collard and his sons Shane, Tyson, and Bill; Rudy Sepulvula, Johnny Valencia, Steve Grigalva, Richard Rodriguez, Mike Eby, and, last but not least, the venerable Patsy Eby. They kept us in the saddle and on the range so we could truly experience a cowboy's life.

Library of Congress Cataloging-in-Publication Data

Anderson, Joan.
    Cowboys: roundup on an American ranch / text by Joan Anderson; photographs by George Ancona.
       p.   cm.
    Summary: A pictorial essay on cowboys, focusing on the annual roundup at the Eby Ranch in Faywood, New Mexico.
    ISBN 0-590-48424-9
    1. Cowboys — West (U.S.) — Juvenile literature. 2. Cowboys — New Mexico — Juvenile literature. 3. Eby family — Juvenile literature. 4. West (U.S.) — Social life and customs — Juvenile literature. 5. New Mexico — Social life and customs — Juvenile literature. 6. Cowboys — West (U.S.) — Pictorial works — Juvenile literature. 7. Cowboys — New Mexico — Pictorial works — Juvenile literature. [1. Eby family. 2. Cowboys. 3. Ranch life — New Mexico. 4. New Mexico — Social life and customs.] I. Ancona, George, ill. II. Title.
    F596.A55 1996
    978 — dc20   95-8866
    CIP
    AC

12 11 10 9 8 7 6 5 4 3 2 1   6 7 8 9/9 0 1/0

Printed in Singapore   46

First printing, March 1996

Designed by Marijka Kostiw

The text type was set in Garth Graphic and Copperplate Heavy by WLCR New York, Inc.
The display type was set in Retablo Regular from RXC Design.

¡MUCHAS GRACIAS!

TO HENRY TORRES

WHO INTRODUCED US

TO THE WORLD OF

RANCHING AND COWBOYING.

*C*lank. *Clank. Clank.* The windmill catches an early morning breeze, spitting water into a tank. Horses nicker and snort, sticking their noses over the rickety fence. Coyotes whine at the setting moon just as the black sky turns a dark blue. It's a chilly six o'clock in the morning at the Eby Ranch in Faywood, New Mexico.

Leedro and Colter Eby, ages thirteen and eleven, are up as fast as jackrabbits. They pull on their long johns, button up their flannel shirts, and climb into blue jeans and canvas jackets, clothes meant to protect them from ragged brush and cactus needles. They haven't been going to school for the last two weeks. It's spring roundup, and their dad, Larry Eby, has needed their help to find all eight hundred cattle that graze on the seventy-five-square-mile territory — and drive them into the ranch.

Still groggy, the boys pass through the kitchen as they head for the jeep, not stopping for even a bite of breakfast. "We feed the horses before anyone else," says Leedro. "We wouldn't have the ranch if it weren't for them."

Driving down the mile-long road leading from their house to the ranch, they dodge roadrunners and antelope that dart across their path. "I like the early mornin' best," Leedro says, his breath making vapor as it hits the cold air. "Everything's fresh. There's a whole day ahead, full of things to do."

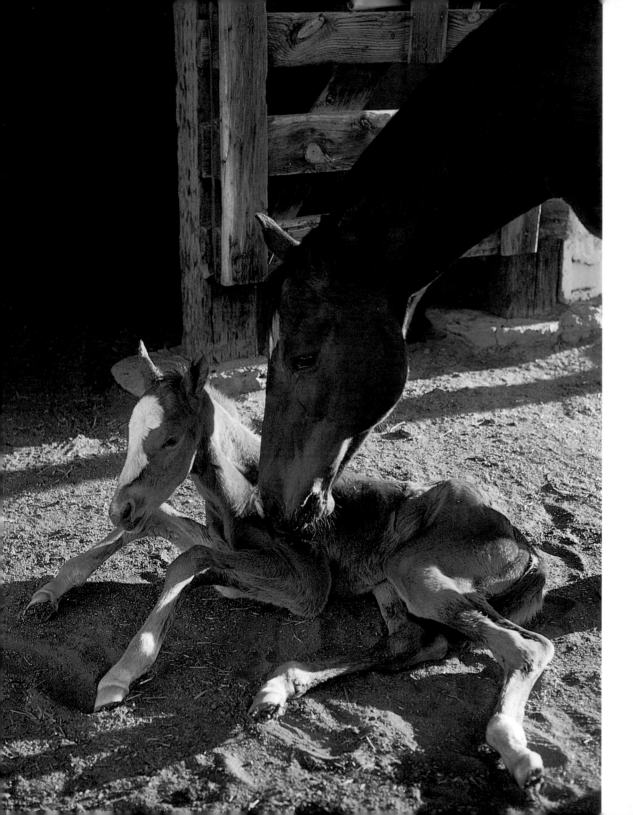

A few minutes later, Leedro's foot hits the brake, and the jeep comes to a halt beside the barn. The boys' grandma, Patsy Eby, is waiting for them.

"Look'it here," she says, gushing like a new mother. "Rebel's had her baby, just an hour ago. Isn't she precious?"

The boys gape at the skinny little foal. But there's no time to
dawdle. They head for the hayloft, where Leedro lugs bales off
the pile into a wheelbarrow. He pushes it toward the corral, where
his brother snips the string around the bales and spreads the feed
evenly around the pen.

Patsy is pleased to be relieved of some of the heavy chores.
Ranch-raised herself, she has been a cowgirl all her life, "ridin' a
horse as good as any man," she says. "You can't go to school and
learn to be a cowboy. You're just born to it. Rose Ann and Larry
have had the boys in the saddle since they were babies. You either
take to it, or you don't."

The horizon changes from pink to orange as the sun pops over the red clay cliffs. Clouds of dust rise from the dirt road as a string of pickups barrel into the ranch.

Hired for the roundup, eight cowboys with bowlegs and leathery faces climb out of the trucks. With steaming cups of coffee in hand, they saunter toward the corral. Some lug their heavy saddles, while others coax their horses out of trailers. They come with sons, daughters, and sometimes wives, all eager to do what was bred into them.

"We was all brought up ridin' cow-horses, workin' with cattle," says one cowboy with the same slow drawl he uses to coax the animals he works with. "All of us has a lot of cow in him. We've been around cattle so long, we just know 'em."

The smell of saddle soap and neat's-foot oil, used to keep saddle leather soft, permeates the air. The cowboys haul saddles and blankets out of the tack room. They brush the snarls out of their horses' backs and speak tenderly to them.

"There's no vehicle that can go where these horses go," says Leedro, pulling the saddle strap tight, making sure the rigging has no extra play. "They give us so much. We've got to take care of 'em."

Just then he notices his horse favoring her hind leg. He rubs his hand gently over her ankle. It feels hot. "You're not goin' any-where," he says, realizing she must have strained a tendon on yes-terday's ride. "You need a couple days' rest." He pats her neck and leads her back to a pen.

The once-tranquil corral is now alive. Boots pound the hardened earth, and spurs clink as the cowboys head for their horses, hiding bridles behind their backs.

"The horses don't like no bridle on," says Leedro, "so we kinda creep up on 'em."

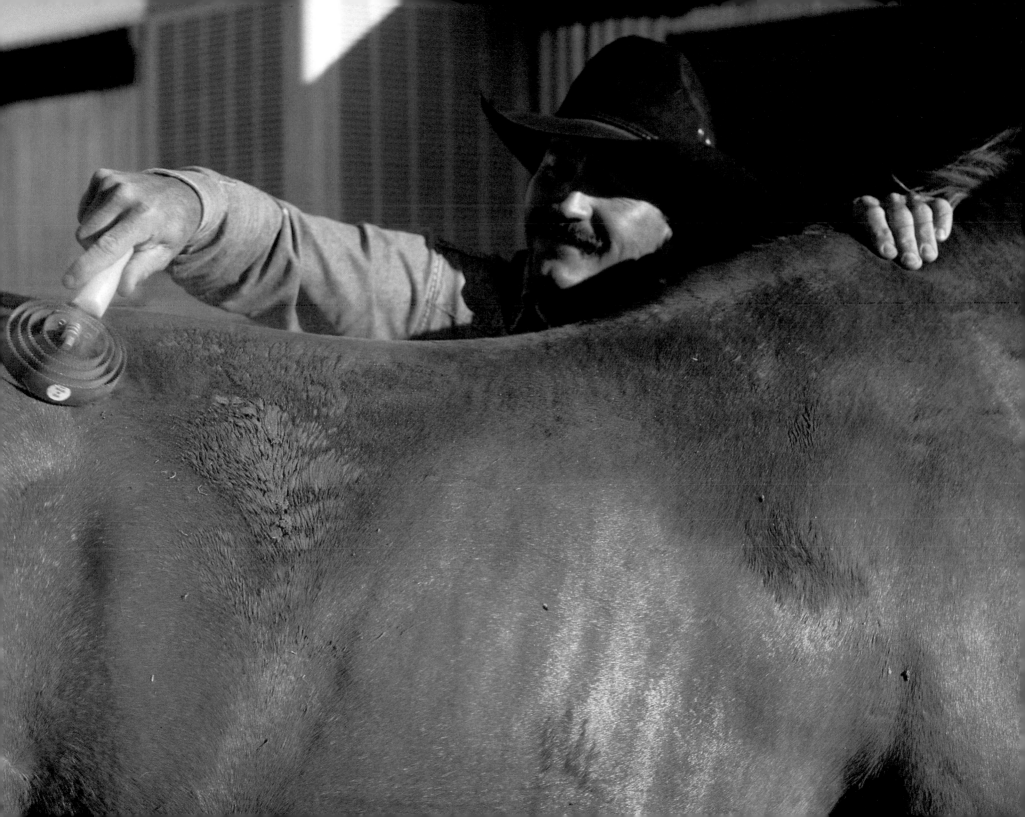

Meanwhile, experienced horse trainer Randy Biebelle has cornered the high-spirited filly that he's been breaking for the past thirty days. All eyes are on Randy to see how he handles her. He talks gently to the barely tame horse. After some initial balking, she lets him secure the bit in her mouth.

"I think you're ready to ride," Randy says, patting her and swiftly saddling her up. "We'll soon see," he says, thinking ahead to the challenge of riding her all day. Just then the horse bucks, as if to assert that she's still free.

All the cowboys are mounted and ready to go when Leedro and Colter's mom, Rose Ann, pulls up. She tucks freshly made burritos into saddlebags and grabs the reins of her horse, Tommy. A full-fledged cowgirl herself, Rose Ann would rather work alongside her husband and boys than stay behind.

"Time to head out," Larry says. The cowboys gather for their orders, some still shivering in the cool early-morning air. It's been a dry winter and an even drier spring. Larry is anxious to sell off as many cows as he can before he loses them to the drought.

Larry has divided up his territory into sections like a checkerboard. Each cowboy is assigned a section, where he will search for and bring in every last grazing cow.

"Leedro, you head east up the canyon. Colter, you go with Johnny and Abe. The rest of you come with me to the high country. See you at Tom Brown Basin in a couple of hours." They trot off toward the red clay mesas, into the wind, eyes squinting to avoid the dust, felt hats pulled down around their ears. The lilt of voices bounces off the canyon walls for a time and then fades away.

Leedro feels safe mounted on Comanche, a surefooted horse who can handle rugged terrain. They proceed slowly at first, navigating around craggy mesquite bushes and paddle cactus plants.

Leedro keeps his eyes open for rattlesnakes, knowing horses buck when they see one. The buzz of hummingbirds and the clack of Comanche's hooves against the shale rock keep him company. These wide-open spaces are his backyard, a place he's been playing in and riding over since he was a baby. They pass rock caves where Apaches corralled their horses, spots where his dad found weapons left behind by Spanish conquistadores, and rock carvings drawn by Mimbres Indians.

Seconds later his horse stops. She neighs and jumps backward. Leedro looks around to see what is upsetting her. Nearby lies a dead baby calf, probably killed by a hungry predator. Coyotes and mountain lions, desperate for food when there is a drought, ravage anything they can find. Leedro has never seen conditions this bad on the range, and he's worried.

On the other side of the mountain, Larry Eby stares at the brown rubble that was once hearty food for his cattle. He is concerned about the health of his herd as well as the condition of his land.

As he rides, he scans the quiet hills for signs of life, cows grazing or the movement of deer and antelope. It takes a while to find the cattle with Larry's method of ranching. "I spread 'em out, only about eight or ten on each section. That way I'm bein' kinder to the land. It does take a little longer to round 'em up." But Larry doesn't mind.

"Comin' up here, smellin' the sage, breathin' clean air, I forget about everything back in the valley.

"I love this place," he says of the ranch his family has worked for one hundred fifty years. "My dad used to say that you didn't need church when you lived out here under the big sky — you can see God's been here." Even so, Larry would feel much better if the sky turned dark with rain clouds.

The cowboys usually begin to spot cows after about an hour of riding. "It's like findin' a needle in a haystack," Leedro says. "You gotta think like a cow. What would they be feedin' on? Where would they be hidin' their newborns? If they finished breakfast, would they be sleepin' under trees by the waters?"

Just then he sees a momma with a newborn close beside, fur still damp, legs unsteady. Leedro smiles. The new life makes up for the animal that didn't make it.

"When you finally start collectin' them," Leedro continues, "it takes a lot of cow jibberish to get 'em movin'. Hey, hey, hey, yup, yup, c'mon girlie, git up there," he hollers and then prods them with a stick or taps them with his lasso until they get going.

"There's a time to rush a cow and a time to be slow with her. A cowboy's got to know which way a cow's goin' to run, and the shortest way to head her off."

It doesn't take long after finding the first cow to have a string of ten or twelve. The trick is to push them along and together.

Just when the riding gets lonely, Leedro spots his dad up above him on a mesa ledge. He hears a whistle and looks below. Randy is chasing a frisky yearling who doesn't want to stay with the others.

"Head 'em off," Larry shouts, just as a heifer breaks free and follows the yearling. Leedro charges after Randy as his dad gallops down from the mesa in hopes of blocking them from straying too far. Before long, half the team is in the chase, six cowboys running after two cows. Three miles and forty-five minutes later, they finally lasso the skittish runaways and drag them back to the rest of the herd.

What can start out as a short day frequently turns into a long one. "You can never tell when they'll break up on you," Leedro says. "You can have a real smooth drive goin', and then somethin' will happen. They'll get spooked, or a bull will get ornery, and boom, they just take off."

Now the fun begins. Each cowboy on his own has found ten or twenty head of cattle, and they are slowly, cautiously moving them toward one of the many corrals that dot the range. With combined herds, the cowboys begin pushing fifty or sixty cows, trying to keep them together even though each cow has a favorite direction.

"There was a stampede down on the flats last week," Leedro says, a smile in his eyes. "The cows are kinda wild there in the open spaces. They don't like bein' bunched and driven. Sure enough, as we neared the pen the lead cow took off. Colter and I followed her, ridin' forever to catch up, when the other cows got the same idea. They went in the opposite direction. We had cows goin' everywhere, hats flyin' off, dust swirlin' . . . all you could hear were poundin' hooves and cowboys yellin'."

Just before noon, half of the cowboys are at a corral called The Box, where they lead the cattle into a pen and close the gate.

They refresh themselves near a windmill, which creaks and rattles as the wind catches its blades and water pours into the tank. As the horses eagerly slurp, Leedro takes off his jacket and grabs his canteen for a drink. It feels good to stop. The corral, tucked between giant rocks and steep embankments, is a cool place to rest from the blazing sun.

These watering spots are vital for the cattle, who are struggling to survive and raise their young. The Ebys have seventeen windmills that pump water up from underground springs. Since the forty natural water holes and creek beds have dried up in the drought, the windmills must be kept in perfect working order if the animals are to survive.

After ten minutes or so, Larry gives the order to move out. "We can't keep the others waitin'," he says, referring to the rest of the crew on the other side of the mountain. Leedro opens the pen containing the newly herded cows, and they rush out, their heavy bodies rubbing up against each other, dust clouds rising from the weight of their hooves. They look confused and angry about being pushed and prodded. One utters a long "moo" and then another, until a chorus of guttural groans fills the valley that was once silent.

"C'mon, girlie, thataway," a cowboy coaxes a big fat momma. "Yo bully, git up there."

This time the cattle are compliant. It only takes half an hour to drive them to Tom Brown, an enormous basin scooped out of the barren landscape. Eyes squinting, the cowboys scan the hills for signs of the rest of the crew. Randy points east, spotting Rose Ann's blue shirt. Leedro sees Colter herding a bunch of cows through a thicket. The hills are now dotted with cowboys leading strings of cattle toward the valley.

And then the cowboys emerge from all directions, proceeding gently, quietly toward the center, each string of cattle becoming like the spoke of a wheel. Larry gallops out ahead to count the cows and determine if the crew has found them all. A good cowman knows precisely how many cows he has in every section of his land. After a quick calculation, Larry shakes his head in amazement. "You got 'em all," he shouts above the bawling. "Let's move 'em out."

The drive is on. "Keep 'em together," Larry shouts above the thunder of hooves. The point is to gather cattle, not scatter them. "It's like keepin' a bunch of marbles on the table," Larry says as he prods them into line.

"Yippee!" Colter shouts, twirling his rope and lassoing first one calf and then another, more for his own amusement than anything else. "Once you get 'em goin' forward, you don't want 'em goin' back," he says.

The cows duck and dodge, startled by the slightest diversion. In order to keep them together, several cowboys ride swing, along the sides of the herd, to keep the line from bulging. Larry rides point, up front, heading them to the next watering place. Colter, Leedro, and their friends and mom ride flank, behind, staring at rear ends and getting most of the dust in their faces.

Even so, this part of the roundup is fun. After hours of riding alone, whistling to themselves, the cowboys can now talk to one another, munch on burritos, and drink soda.

Today they must push the cattle to a branding pen, where the cowboys will burn the Eby brand onto the hide of more than a hundred calves.

Two men have gone ahead to ready the fire and heat up the branding irons.

"We try to make it painless," Larry says, never wanting his cattle to be under stress. "But brandin's an important part of ranchin'."

If a cow wanders into another rancher's territory, the mark on the cow's backside tells just who owns her. The Eby brand has been passed on from generation to generation. It's like the family crest.

When the herd reaches the pen, the mommas and babies are separated from the rest and led into a large corral. They huddle in a corner, bawling and mooing.

Colter gallops into the ring, lasso flying, and ropes the first subject by the head. He drags the calf toward the center, where the other cowboys stand ready to perform specific tasks. Not a word is spoken. Each person knows exactly what is expected of him.

Two of the cowboys throw the calves down and hold them steady, while another presses the red-hot iron into the cow's hide. Rose Ann stands ready to inject them with medicine to keep them free of disease. The male calves are castrated, and they all have their ears tagged. It takes but a minute or two to accomplish all this before releasing the little creature, who scampers back to his anxious momma.

There's the smell of burning flesh and the grunts of men holding down strong-willed animals. It is challenging and exhausting work, and when the job is done, the cowboys take a moment to celebrate.

Dog tired, the crew finally heads home after a twelve-hour day. Leedro and Colter wish they could settle in front of the television, but they know better. Tomorrow is the final push — when all eight hundred head are herded into the ranch itself. There are chores to be done to prepare for the arrival of so many cows in the corral.

"No jobs on a ranch are one-man jobs," Leedro says. "When my mom or dad asks me to help, I know they can't do it alone." Whether it's fixing fence or hauling hay, someone has to drive the truck, unload the goods, stand ready to assist.

And so Rose Ann, Larry, Colter, and Leedro work more long hours. They clean the water troughs and deliver fresh hay to the holding pen, preparing for the anxious cattle that have been on the move for days.

Shipping day begins long before dawn. Cows move better if they are driven before they eat. The lead cow, eager to be left alone to graze, hurries toward the smell of the grain and hay that await her at the ranch corral.

Once the cows are locked inside the pen, the cowboys must identify and separate both the mommas and babies. The babies are too young to be sold, and they will be sent back to pasture for another year of fattening up. It is the hefty yearlings that will be shipped and sold. They are separated, male from female.

Looking like bullfighters, other cowboys, holding long wands, cajole and prod the yearlings as they are separated. Then they are weighed and quickly ushered into the shipping trucks, and off they go.

"You learn early that we raise 'em to sell 'em," Leedro says, sitting on the fence with his brother as the truck pulls away. "You have to accept it, but it still hurts."

Weatherbeaten and dusty, the cowboys lean against the fence, lips cracked, bodies sore, faces stained by dusty sweat. Drinks come out of the cooler, and the kids run off to play stickball.

Rose Ann and Patsy lay out a spread of Mexican food, and the cowboys relax and revel in the memory of the roundup. "There ain't nothin' better," says one. "I've tried workin' different jobs, but there's nothin' as good as bein' a cowboy. It's a good, clean life. Even the dirt is clean."

Almost nothing could move these cowboys now. But in a wink, there is a swirl of wind. A dark cloud moves over a nearby mesa. A roll of thunder is followed by a crackle of lightning.

And then it begins — blessed rain, pounding fierce and loud against the rock-hard red soil, creating rivers in the corral. No one runs for cover. Instead, they put on the yellow slickers they've been waiting to wear. It will need to rain for a while to do any good, but for now, the Ebys are grateful.

It's been a long two weeks, but the roundup has been a successful one. The rain makes it even better. "My dad used to say that if you had to buy the rain, it'd cost you a million dollars," Larry says. "I don't ever want to forget to say thank you." ♘

GLOSSARY